Make Friends

by L. L. Owens
illustrated by Chris Davidson

Content Consultant
M. A. Brennan
Assistant Professor, Community Development
Department of Family, Youth, and Community Sciences
University of Florida

visit us at www.abdopublishing.com

Published by Magic Wagon, a division of the ABDO Group, 8000 West 78th Street, Edina, Minnesota 55439. Copyright © 2011 by Abdo Consulting Group, Inc. International copyrights reserved in all countries. All rights reserved. No part of this book may be reproduced in any form without written permission from the publisher.

Looking Glass Library™ is a trademark and logo of Magic Wagon.

Printed in the United States of America, North Mankato, Minnesota.
012010
092010

Text by L. L. Owens
Illustrations by Chris Davidson
Edited by Mari Kesselring
Interior layout and design by Becky Daum
Cover design by Becky Daum

Library of Congress Cataloging-in-Publication Data
Owens, L. L.
  Make friends / by L.L. Owens ; illustrated by Chris Davidson ; content consultant M. A. Brennan.
      p. cm. — (Let's be social)
  Includes index.
  ISBN 978-1-60270-802-0
  1. Friendship—Juvenile literature. I. Davidson, Chris, 1974- II. Title.

  BF575.F66O94 2011
  177'.62—dc22
                                        2009048356

Table of Contents

What Are Friends?

All people have friends. Everyone *is* a friend, too! But what does it mean to be a friend?

Friends are people you care about. They are important. There are many different kinds of friends.

Grace and Jessica are friends. They like to spend time together, and they share interests. Grace and Jessica both enjoy reading.

Grace and Jessica make each other laugh. They stand up for each other. And they help each other during good times and bad times. They are good friends.

Learn to say "friend" in a different language:

amigo (Spanish)   *kawan* (Indonesian)
tomodachi (Japanese) *freund* (German)
vriend (Afrikaans)   *ami* (French)

Types of Friends

There are many different types of friends. One kind of friend is a casual friend. Ryan only sees his casual friends once in a while. He has a few casual friends in his weekend karate class. He also has a friend named Juan who lives far away. Juan is a casual friend because Ryan only talks to him a few times a year.

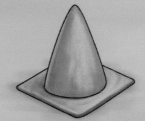

Luis and Dan are close friends. They see each other often. They know each other well. Luis and Dan have a lot in common. They both love talking about dinosaurs.

Most people only have a few close friends. It takes time to get to know a close friend.

Jeremiah and Aidan are best friends. They share the same ideas about most things. Jeremiah and Aidan do not agree on everything, though. If they did, the friendship would be boring.

Jeremiah and Aidan can always be themselves with each other. They love doing many of the same things. They will have a good time together no matter what they do.

Many people have more than one best friend.

Best friends, like all types of friends, can change. Jeremiah and Aidan were best friends in second grade. In third grade, they both made new best friends. But Jeremiah and Aidan are still good friends. They try to stay open to all new friendships.

Sometimes Mia hangs out with more than one friend at a time. She likes to see friends in groups. On Mia's birthday, all of her friends came to her house. She had fun hanging out with all of her friends at once.

Friends get together to celebrate holidays and other special events throughout the year.

Meeting Friends

Andy finds new friends everywhere.
They live in his neighborhood. They go to
his school. For some kids, meeting new
friends is easy and fun.

Sometimes Andy feels shy about making
friends. He remembers that not everyone
will end up being his friend. But he has
lots of kids to choose from!

19

Jada meets new friends in her dance class.
Meeting a new friend starts the same way as
meeting anyone else. Jada smiles and says hello.
She introduces herself. Then she asks questions
to get to know her new friends.

Being a Friend

When Amal and his friend Joel hang out, they do all sorts of things. They talk or play basketball. They eat pizza or watch movies. They use the computer or listen to music. Amal has fun doing things with Joel.

Sometimes friends are related
to each other. Siblings, parents,
grandparents, and other family
members make great friends.

Carlos and Matt have a good time together. The best thing about being friends is that they can trust each other. They must respect each other to earn that trust. Respect and trust help make their friendship last.

Friends also look out for each other. Carlos stands up for Matt when he is being teased. Matt helps Carlos when he needs him, too.

Sam and Kayla are best friends. Sometimes they get mad at each other. That's okay! Because they are friends, they will work it out. They will say that they are sorry. And they will always forgive each other. Sam and Kayla like each other too much to stay mad for long.

Good friends help each other through hard times. They also celebrate each other's good news. Friends keep their promises. They stay loyal to each other. In a good friendship, both friends tell the truth and support each other. Everyone needs friends!

Friend Project

Choose your favorite quote from below. Make a colorful poster to show the quote's meaning. When you're finished, give the poster to one of your friends.

"I get by with a little help from my friends."
—*The Beatles*

"Who finds a faithful friend, finds a treasure."
—*Jewish saying*

"With clothes the new are best. With friends the old are best."
—*Chinese saying*

"Hold a true friend with both your hands."
—*Nigerian saying*

Fun Facts

- Scientists think that all human beings have a basic need to make friends.

- *Charlotte's Web* is a classic friendship tale. The book focuses on the friendship between a girl named Fern and a pig named Wilbur.

- George Washington and Benjamin Franklin were friends.

Glossary

casual—relating to someone you know only slightly.

introduce—to make yourself known to someone else by telling him or her your name.

loyal—faithful to someone or something.

respect—to show consideration and thoughtfulness.

sibling—a brother or a sister.

support—to help and encourage someone.

On the Web

To learn more about friends, visit ABDO Group online at **www.abdopublishing.com**. Web sites about friends are featured on our Book Links page. These links are routinely monitored and updated to provide the most current information available.

Index